THE STING IN THE TALE

POEMS AND SHORT STORIES

BY

JEAN HILL

ABOUT ME

About Me ... What can I say? I'm your typical Mrs Average really. I'm wife to Robin, Mum to daughters, Deborah and Sharon, and Granny to Benjamin, Samantha and Jamie. I'm sister, auntie, mother-in-law, friend ... all this come first, second and third, and I love them all to bits.

I'm not clever – can't boast of ever reading the classics or going to University – I went to an East Acton Secondary Modern School in the 50's which, even in those days, dealt mainly with riot control rather than teaching and, at fourteen, was sent to learn to type.

I hate pretension – can't stand the ballet – only listen to the lightest classical music - and have never been to Ascot in my life (even though it's only down the road). I listen to Radio 2, read the tabloids, think Pam Ayes is wonderful and watch Coronation Street – see ... a real Mrs Average – although probably pretty street-wise!

I love animals passionately. I enjoy nature - to walk in meadows, forests, snow-capped mountains and around lakes with Robin (who still holds my hand) is my idea of heaven. I love adventure and travelling and new experiences in far flung places. Never let old age take away the joy of living and always stand on your own soap-box! And ... when the muse sits on my shoulder the words flow and poetry fills my head, I become ME. And then I feel ....

Some of my poems and stories will make you laugh but some will make you cry. Thank-you for reading them.

Jean Hill

I'm keeping my brain active
I don't think it will shrivel
Because here I sit with pen in hand
Writing all this drivel!

ACKNOWLEDGEMENTS

Deborah and **Samantha** … for being so hugely supportive in the practical production of this book.
Without your skill and patience it would never have happened.

Sharon … for being the provider of my initial inspiration.

Robin … for being my human spell-checker.

Benjamin and **Jamie** … for just being …….

THANK – YOU ALL

Contents

Poems   **Page 6**

Short Stories   **Page 86**

Poems

INTERNET DATE

I've down-loaded all the photos
His six-pack clear to see
A hunk of pure testosterone
And they've reserved him – just for me

He's tall and dark and solvent
He's all a man should be
Athletic, fit and sexy
With a university degree

So I'm off to our first meeting
The future's looking bright
The agency's assured me
That he's my Mr Right

I'm tarted to the eyebrows
Shaved my legs and done my hair
I've plastered on the war-paint
Agonised on what to wear

We're meeting in the chip shop
To get to know each other
Will it lead to wedding bells
Or be my illicit lover

Bloody Hell! I see him in the flesh
He's aged some twenty years
The only hair upon his head
Is sprouting out his ears

The teeth seen on the photograph
Are his – all white and straight
In reality they're tombstones
On a wonky fitting plate

He's tattoos up his arm-pits
Has piercings I can't mention
Wrinkled; past his sell-by date
And about to draw his pension

There's a straining of shirt buttons
And he's wearing "grandad" braces
He's so fat I can't make out
Exactly where his waist is

Flab overhangs his collar
Hairy, pulpy, sweaty, pink
And to a Neanderthal
He must be the missing link

He's podgy sausage fingers
And a wart upon his nose
God forbid he takes his shoes off
I'm sure he's got webbed toes

His hobby is train-spotting
Wears a nerdy anorak
To fancy him I'd have to be
A nymphomaniac

He still lives with his mother
And he wears his socks in bed
And he wants a little woman
Someone docile he can wed

But I can tell you here and now
That I won't join his clan
He reminds me of the hunch-back
Ringing bells in Notre Dame

I'm asking for a refund
I won't be his paramour
The jerk said he was forty-one
But he's really sixty-four

I know from our first meeting
Real romance won't come soon
I'll console myself with chocolate bars
And stick to Mills and Boon

LEVELS OF EQUALITY

I don't want to be a man
With mucky jobs to do
I'll happily cook the dinner
While he unblocks the loo

Do I want to change a wheel?
With hands all greasy, blacked
No, I'll play the dumbest blonde
With finger-nails Shellacked

It's good to be a teacher
And an architect is fine
To be a 'brickie' with a hod
Is where I draw the line

We've lovely lady doctors
And clever surgeons too
We've pilots sporting pony-tails
And judges – quite a few

We've solicitors and scientists
All of the female gender
But I'd prefer a burly copper
Arresting thugs out on a bender

I like it when a gentleman
Holds open doors for me
I think it's called 'good manners'
And I'll thank him prettily

I don't want your feminism
It's been taken much too far
If that's what's called equality
You can burn it with your bra

We know we're more than equal
Brains plus beauty cannot fail
Take the best and leave the mess
To the poor old Alpha Male

SHOPPING

There's a stigma over shopping
Some say Waitrose is the best
They think customers of ASDA
All wear flat caps and string vests

With the purchase of newspapers
Derision goes beyond the pale
Why do readers of the Telegraph
Mock those who read the Mail?

Me – I bargain hunt in Poundland
I'm financially astute
And you can keep your Harrods bags
Mine's full of Primark loot

I like to shop at Lidl's
And then I'll have a treat
I'll scoff their half-price chocolate bars
Watching Coronation Street

CLASS ACT

There are those born with a silver spoon
Who are arrogant – bombastic
But for the vast majority
Our spoons are made of plastic

If with veneered superiority
You show others veiled disdain
They'll see through your hypocrisy
And you'll have just yourself to blame

So whether prince or pauper
No matter rich or poor
Let's work together to promote
Classless 'esprit de corps'

MEDICAL OPTIONS

When you phone our doctor
Wanting medical advice
You connect to an answer-phone
A multi-functional device

There's a variety of options
And important is your call
You've choices number one to five
But must listen to them all

Press number one and wait a while
For a non-serious condition
Example: if you're over-weight
And need the dietician

If your symptoms are non-threatening
It's number two for all things trivial
Then you're treated to nice music
Therapeutic and convivial

For anything more worrying
Press three and hold the line
If it's just a simple body rash
Ring off – try calamine

If your temperature is rising
And you need the duty-nurse
Take aspirin or press number four
So your symptoms don't get worse

And if you've reached your final breath
But feel you're still alive
Try to summon up the strength
And press button number five

But if you think you're at death's door
And about to meet your maker
Press the "hash" and then hang up
And phone the undertaker

WINDMILL THIEF

My husband built a windmill
In blue and green and red
It ornaments the garden
By a beautiful rose bed

By night there came some burglars
In a van of limey-green
But, by a caring neighbour
They were disturbed and seen

So they smashed up my windmill
Threw the pieces all around
They stamped upon the yellow sails
And left them on the ground

Now my love's re-built the windmill
But I need a deterrent
I'm fearful thieves may come again
It's scary and repellent

Perhaps a ring of rusty wire
Barbed with sharpened facets
But it's a shame, it's not allowed
To prick a burglar's assets

Because the police would question *me*
"Did you put the barbed-wire there?"
What me, Oh No, of course not
I wouldn't harm a hair

"Then could it be your husband
Was it he who did it
Did he cause that injury
To the thieving bugger's digit?"

We don't know who put it there
The outcome is quite tragic
It must have been the fairies
Who put it there – by magic!

GONE FROM ME

They diagnosed dementia
And I don't know how to cope
There's no chance she will recover
An existence without hope

The children all spoke sadly
Saying "It's too much for you, Dad"
And so we put her in a home
And I miss the life we had

With nursing staff professional
I think she's treated kindly
But now she's institutionalised
And follows orders blindly

They've dressed her in a flowery frock
Her cardigan's inside-out
Mis-matched clothes I know aren't hers
They're all mixed up – no doubt

Her slippers on the wrong feet
Secured by frayed Velcro
She sits and smiles quite vacantly
With others – in a row

Where is my love who once was
My wife, busy, smart and wise
She's in a world where I can't reach
Confusion fills her eyes

So each day I sit beside her
Heart anguished, filled with dread
I hold her hand and comfort her
She's gone but she's not dead

And now the nurse approaches
My visit's over for the day
She tucks a rug around my love
And then wheels her away

WHERE IS GOD?

Where is God in conflict?
Is he witness to our grief?
Think back to the holocaust
To shatter your belief

Was he with them in the chambers?
Did he watch them gassed and die?
Did he show benevolent mercy?
Hear the choking children's cry?

Did he still the hand that slaughtered?
Did he smite the evil down?
Does he watch the people's terror?
As in their own blood they drown

And still the wars are raging
And the innocents still die
If there's a Heavenly Father
It's time someone questioned Why?

GRANNY IN THE MIRROR

Where is that girl of seventeen
With bouffant hair and style
Who tottered on stiletto heels
And always had a smile

Once I had nice bosoms
All firm and round and neat
Now they're pendulous and drooping
And heading South towards my feet

I look into the mirror
And see mounds of fatty slack
I glare at the reflection
And my Granny glares straight back

I still try hard to "strut-my-stuff"
But my bladder muscle's lax
And my confidence comes with Tena
In discreet little packs

My stockings should be surgical
To help veins varicosed
But I still wear a skimpy thong
Beneath sheer panti-hose

I've got to wear a hearing aid
But please feel free to shout
I'd like to join the conversation
But I often feel left out

I know I've lost my figure
And now I tend to nap
As I sit and watch the telly
And my tum sits on my lap

But I'm keeping up the diet
And it's lettuce for my tea
So one day there in the mirror
Granny's vanished and there's me

I've tried to stay quite trendy
To be "me" the way I am
But there's always some frump out there
Saying "Mutton Dressed as Lamb"

When was it that I became old
I don't recall the day
A thief called "time" crept quietly by
And stole my youth away

I don't feel any different
In my heart I'm still that girl
And get me on the dance floor
I will spin and twist and twirl

That girl of seventeen's still there
I can feel her spirit free
That wrinkly mirror image
Is my Granny; it's not me

MOURN

When in the church the vicar says
"Together we are drawn
To celebrate the life of ….."
No, we're not, we're here to mourn

All life's a celebration
From the time of your first breath
But please don't 'celebrate' a life
When it's time to 'mourn' a death

On this one sad occasion
When by tradition black is worn
We've done with celebrating
Comfort me, together, mourn

TAX CODES

I've just received new tax codes
From the Inland Revenue
Any every year they get it wrong
They haven't got a clue

The basic rate - twenty per cent
Of my income – and I say
I don't earn that much money
From the work that comes my way

If I work odd part-time hours
My pension to eke out
I get all different tax codes
And my tax goes up the spout

If I earn below tax threshold
And little extra jobs I juggle
It's quite beyond the tax man
And he gets into a muddle

I try to sort it on the phone
But speak to their machines
My call's important to them
Oh Yeah! In your dreams

So I'll present facts and figures
In a clear and concise way
Work out to the penny
What, and if, I have to pay

I'll calculate my income tax
Overcome bureaucracy
They can stuff their bloody tax codes
I'm a Tax Free OAP

CRIMINAL ESCALATION

There are thugs and yobs and hooligans
Causing havoc on estates
They haunt our city centres
With a gang of feral mates

There's litter louts and vandals
Menacing and criminal
Shop-lifters and boy-racers
Their punishment is minimal

We don't want graffiti on our walls
Or meet hoodies out to fight
We want our homes protected
And sleep peacefully at night

If they're not stopped in their tracks
They go on to become
Burglars, muggers, robbers
And serious criminal scum

Perpetrators of all major crimes
Start out as little fish
Net them early – hit them hard
Is our law-abiding wish

From minor crime to major
Is just one little hop
We need bobbies on the beat
To stem trouble – make it stop

If at last to court they're taken
They say "It ain't fair, m'lud"
Show them zero tolerance
And nip it in the bud

Please don't cut back on policing
Of the minor nuisance crimes
Stop criminal escalation
The plague of modern times

LIFE'S COLOURS

Cowards are all called Yellow
In the dumps you could be Blue
And when you're feeling sickly
Then you turn a Greenish hue

With rage you could be Purple
With embarrassment turn Red
And finally you turn to Grey
They're your ashes – and you're dead!

LIGHTS

I love the light the stars shine through
A midnight sky of navy blue
I love the lights on winter trees
The diamond glitter when they freeze

I love the lights of towns so busy
On fairground rides that make you dizzy
I love the light – warm sunshine rays
Illuminating summer days

But most of all I love to see
The car's headlights bringing him to me

ETHNICITY

Why are folks so bothered
About ethnicity
People are just people
And they're all the same to me

Some are black and some are brown
And there are those I've seen
When out on a drinking binge
Turn a sickly shade of green

There are those that we call yellow
And a variety of white
But we all end up looking grey
In dawn or dusk half-light

In every race and culture
Most are nice but a few who
Pursue a life of evil
Don't judge all by what they do

We are all human beings
And if you stop to think
Universally our blood is red
Me – I'm blotchy and pale pink

Just accept the differences
Let no prejudice deflect
We share a life on this old earth
Show mutual respect

We don't have to *love* our neighbour
Just be tolerant and kind
Show compassion for each other
Leave animosity behind

Forget which God you worship
If your hair is straight or curled
Let's live in peace together
And make this a better world

TO MY DEAREST DAUGHTER

I didn't want to buy you
A card from any shop
With words composed by others
Which just don't mean a lot

I simply want to tell you
How much you mean to me
And how I love you dearly
Is how it will always be

So on this very special day
So important in your life
You'll always by my daughter
Even though you're now a wife

THE MEANING OF FIVE ALMONDS

One stands for Love
Two is for Health
Three means Fertility
Four is for Wealth

Combine the above
And you will be blessed
With Number Five
Life-Long Happiness

LIBERATE MY FEET

Liberation Day is here my feet
And you're going to smell so sweet
As out of sandals toes will peep
Liberate my feet

Liberation Day is here my toes
The sandal slap on sand echoes
A little pinky toe-nail grows
Liberate my toes

Liberation Day is here my socks
The day sandals come out the box
There is no putting back the clocks
Liberate my socks

Liberation Day for ankle bones
No more pinging of elastic tones
Promise there'll be no more groans
Liberate my bones

Liberation Day is just in time
While I'm so clearly in my prime
Through plastic little toes will shine
Liberation's just fine

Liberation Day is well contrived
Upon the look that I've relied
For my toes there is no where to hide
Liberation world-wide

Liberation will be history
No more polyester socks for me
A new man image you will see
Liberation's mandatory

Liberation's finally arrived
And I'll not mind when I'm deprived
Nearly eighty years my socks survived
Liberation of socks denied

EDITH GOES TO A & E

My name is Edith Peabody
I'm nearly eighty-one
I'm waiting here in A & E
And my bottom's going numb

I've difficulty standing
And sitting I avoid
You can't recline on plastic
With a throbbing haemorrhoid

My blood pressure is rising
And I really need the loo
I want to see the doctor
Before I'm eighty-two

I wish I could go private
And forget the National Health
But I can't get the insurance
And I haven't got the wealth

I've got reflux regurgitation
And water on the knee
And if I sit here much longer
I'll be nearly eighty-three

They're seeing drunks and druggies
And those who like to fight
A & E's become a scary place
And I've been here all night

They're lining up the stretchers
In a draughty corridor
I don't want to meet my maker
Before I'm eighty-four

My toe-nails are in-growing
My bunion's getting worse
My ankles are all swollen
I've not even seen a nurse

I've got creeping rigor-mortis
Am I still alive?
Somebody come and pinch me
If I reach eighty-five

I started with a tickle
Then a deep cough in my chest
I'm sure I've got death rattle
Lurking underneath my vest

I tried to see my GP
My check-up's over-due
But he's gone to fight Ebola
Somewhere in Timbuctoo

So here I wait in A & E
Edith Peabody's my name
Because I've reached my "sell-by" date
I just sit – and don't complain

JOCK MacRAVISH
by MISS LIBERTY BODICE

Jock MacRavish on Hogmanay
In sporran and kilt attired
Went out in search of ladies
On a bicycle he'd hired

He soon espied a buxom lass
And – view it how you like –
They can't charge you with kerb crawling
When you've only got a bike

He said "I'll give you one and six
For an hour of your time"
She said "You've twenty minutes
And the price is one and nine"

Jock counted out the coinage
In the dim light and the gloom
Then she jumped upon his cross-bar
And they raced off to her room

She said "You're past your sell-by date
But I like the look of thee
For you I'll do a BOGOF"
(That's Buy One – Get One Free)

Jock – in the heat of passion – was
Put cruelly to the test
He had trouble with his long-johns
Into which he tucked his vest

But she was fat and ugly
One eye straight and one was tilting
As his blood pressure was rising
He could feel his ardour wilting

He said "You've warts upon your nose
Me impetus is lost
You remind me of a bull-dog
That's been chewing on a wasp"

Jock said "I want a refund
You're well past your prime"
She said "I've got me corsets off
So I'm charging one and nine"

The scene was turning nasty
And Jock reached for his hilt
But tripped upon his sporran
Got his dirk stuck up his kilt

Now the tale of Jock MacRavish
Which we very soon must close
Suffice to say, 'neath his kilt today
Jock wears tartan panti-hose

So – the lesson that Jock learned that night
Visiting Ladies of the Town
You don't get much for one and nine
He now pays half-a-crown

MEDICAL EQUIPMENT SALE

As you suffer wear and tear
With a "sell-by" date expired
Your bodily functions
Leave a lot to be desired

So consult our cut-price catalogue
Spare parts, new and second-hand
From silicone breast implants
To an elastic gastric band

We offer hip replacements
Poly-plastic or titanium
They have a six-month guarantee
With instructions in Romanian

This week's BOGOF offer
(That's Buy One Get One Free)
Will come in very handy
If you've got a dodgy knee

Should you have a pickled liver
Caused by drinking too much wine
We've got a special offer on
For two pounds, ninety-nine

If you've having trouble cardiac
We've a new Chinese pace-maker
With technology advancing
You won't need the undertaker

If you've got a joint that's wonky
And you need to get a spare
We'll send it to you bubble-wrapped
Flown direct by Ryan Air

We've splints and screws and flexi-joints
And pills for traumatism
And for all those into DIY
We've a kit for circumcision

If you've respiratory problems
And with every breath you wheeze
We've some National Health inhalers
They're cheap; they're Taiwanese

We've resuscitation models
That are slightly out of date
We've black and white and unisex
And some that self-inflate

Take time to read our catalogue
You won't find any cheaper
And if you pay us C.O.D
We'll throw in a doctors' bleeper

Our call-centre's based in India
And you can talk direct
To Singh, or Khan or Ahmed
(If you can speak their dialect)

RAINBOW-ROSE

I stare out from this high-rise
There's nothing much to see
Just grim and grey-faced tower blocks
And hopeless poverty

Our flat is always smelly
I think it's called a slum
There's five of us that lives here
Me brothers, me, and Mum

I used to have a Granny
But I don't see her now
She hasn't come to visit
Since she called me Mum a cow

I've got a lot of 'uncles'
And once I had a Dad
But they took him in a police car
For doing something bad

I've got three little brothers
And they're crying to be fed
But there's nothing in the cupboard
And me Mum is still in bed

I love me little brothers
But want someone to love me back
To put their arms around me
And not give me a slap

On the days I go to school
I get a dinner free
I hide some for me brothers
And they have it for their tea

I try to help me brothers
There's Ahmed, he's just five
But he's got impetigo
And with nits his head's alive

My little brother Elvis
He's black, the same as me
He's sores upon his bare backside
He's always wet; he's three

And now we have the baby
He's white and still and 'wrong'
He doesn't cry much anymore
I call him Baby John

Often I am frightened
When I'm alone and cold
I wish I had a friend out there
To give me a hand to hold

Now I'm waiting for 'The Social'
But they've left it far too late
I have a name – it's **Rainbow-Rose**
And next week I'll be **eight**

IF SHE HAD BEEN A BOY

All the mothers that I talk to
Are afflicted just the same
It seems quite universal
Teenage daughters are to blame

So in this open poem
Aimed at all those over ten
Please will you read and digest
As to paper I put pen

Although we love you dearly
And you fill our hearts with pride
Why are you so untidy
With clothes scattered far and wide?

I'd sometimes like to vacuum
If I could find the floor
Knee-deep under rubbish
And spilling out the door

There's paper, broken pencils
Woolly jumpers, dirty tights
Biscuit crumbs and chocolate wrappers
Do you eat in bed all night?

There are lolly-pops and lipsticks
Hair spiky stuff like glue
Old teddy-bears, new tight skirts
Frilly undies all on view

Do you ever shake your duvet
Or put your shoes away
Will you never listen
To a single word I say?

One day I'll gather all your things
And put them in a sack
And you'll have to raid the dustbin
If you want to get them back

But perhaps I should admit it
Daughters can bring joy
But wouldn't life be easier
If she had been a boy

TWO TIMES THIRTY-FIVE

I've just reached three score and ten
It's an awe inspiring day
My reflection in the mirror
Wants to look the other way

I think I need a face-lift
But know that if I do
Surplus skin would surely stretch
From here to Timbuctoo

My laugher lines are crows feet
Between neck and knees I'm sagging
With golden hair now turned to grey
With every year I'm adding

I'd like to lose my cellulite
Or try some liposuction
Or have my stomach stapled
To ensure a weight reduction

I open up my wardrobe doors
And simply stand and stare
Although the clothes are chock-a-block
I've not a thing to wear

Really I should exercise
But even as I sit
The very thought exhausts me
And my leotard won't fit

Sometimes I'm forgetful
My brain not so alert
But I've retained my sense of humour
That's something age can't hurt

So mirror look me in the eye
My age won't be denied
'Cos I'm not really seventy
I'm two times thirty-five

ROUGH JUSTICE

In this far from perfect world
While politicians simply talk
In the streets of towns and cities
You can no longer safely walk

So when you wake up with a headache
And your hair is hanging limp
'Today won't be a good day'
Is the first thing that you think

You poke a finger through your tights
Your bra-strap snaps in two
The toast burns to a cinder
You drop your shower-cap down the loo

The car just coughs and splutters
And the chain's come off your bike
It's no good waiting for a bus
'Cos they've all gone on strike

It's teaming heaven's hard with rain
Your umbrella's inside out
You've a three mile walk before you
When you meet a 'lager lout'

With 'bovver' boots and head all shaved
With arms tattooed, and braces
With broken teeth he soon displays
He's devoid of social graces

"Give us yer money darlin'"
Is his threatening request
You hook the handle of your 'brolly'
In the neck of his string vest

You know he is the final straw
To tip you off the edge
And you land him a good wallop
In his meat and two veg

One always feels much better
Relieved of pent-up frustration
And what a sense of satisfaction
Released on the 'nasties' of this nation

On days that go from bad to worse
If you come across a 'mugger'
Forget about all self-restraint
And slap the thieving bugger

For louts who pick on others
The meek, the frail, the old
To ensure their come-uppance
Is a wonder to behold

True prisoners are the vulnerable
The weak, and frightened, who
Live in fear of crooks and brutes
And the evil things they do

Save your sympathy for the victims
To give them your support
Make the punishment fit the crime
When to justice thugs are brought

DOMINIQUE

If you ever met my husband
Conservative and formal
It wouldn't even cross your mind
That he is far from normal

He's a big-wig on the council
Called James and never Jim
You'd not know that he's a tyrant
And we live in fear of him

I have a baby – Sarah-Jane
Conceived in lust – not love
One day she'll bear the scars of
His cruel hand in velvet glove

I also have a little lad
His name is Tom – he's four
But he's learned to run and hide
As his Dad comes through door

The scenes Tom's had to witness
Reflect in eyes of fear
He shrinks into a corner
Whenever James is here

I've bruises and a broken rib
He never hits me where it shows
Of all his friends and colleagues
There's not a single one that knows

He says that it is all my fault
And it's what I deserved
I frequently can't leave the house
I'm quiet and I'm reserved

I used to be intelligent
Went to university
Now I'm called dull and stupid
A complete nonentity

I wish I could be braver
And catch him unawares
And when he's paralytic
I could push him down the stairs

But my life is one long misery
No chance of retaliation
Daily I'm subjected to
Abject humiliation

I can often see it coming
When he's in a mood and silent
That's the time I shake with fear
For that's when he's most violent

Last night he went mad, berserk
I've black eye, split lip, cut knee
And I hide behind net curtains
So the neighbours cannot see

I need someone to protect us
Who'll help relieve the pain
Is there sanctuary out there
For me and Tom and Sarah-Jane

Dear God, won't you listen
I'm fearful for my life
Please hear my name – it's **Dominique**
And I'm a **battered wife**

I LOVE HIM BECAUSE

When I'm tired he cooks my dinner
Only Cordon Bleu will do
But when he comes to dish it up
It tastes like cut-priced stew

Yesterday he did me lunch
A sardine marinade
But it caught light beneath the grill
We called the fire brigade

Then when I've got a headache
He sends me off to bed
Says, "I'll bring your tea up, dear"
He does – it's jam on bread

And so I climb the stairs some nights
Not wanting hot-sex dramas
Just hot-water-bottle wrapped up round
My winceyette pyjamas

He thinks he is quite macho
But last night in freezing fog
He searched miles for our cat Tiddles
And put his jacket round the dog

And now he's put himself to bed
Not because he's feeling frisky
No, it's because he's caught a cold
Medication is neat whisky

But I know we'll stick together
Faithful, loyal and true
Because when I say "I Love You"
He says "I Love You Too"

TWO SIDES OF CHRISTMAS

Not long ago, nor far away
A child knows not it's Christmas Day
Not for him the games, the toys
No food a-plenty, happy noise

This child lives in a land that's poor
He works from dawn, his hands are sore
Not for him the shirt of silk
No warm bed, no drink of milk

And now we move to another land
With lush green grass and golden sand
Where success is judged by how much money
Truly a land of milk and honey

This child knows it's Christmas Day
With food excessive, friends to play
Computer games, all electronic
Christmas Day – wow – Supersonic!

One child with nothing, one too much
Lord, haven't you heard of 'Going Dutch'
Consider not the race, the creed
Laugher, love, and food, all need

I do not mean to criticize
One all-powerful, one all-wise
But look upon this imperfection
Perhaps, Oh Lord, a small correction?

MY WAY

I'm not afraid of being dead
But I am afraid of dying
Don't want resuscitation when
On my death-bed I am lying

Don't hook me up with wires and tubes
Don't lengthen my demise
I want to dignify my death
Before I'm tranquilised

So I've stock-piled pills and potions
And when my life is done
I'll leave this world by my own hand
Goodbye – With Love - From Mum

DREAM THIN

Potatoes crisp roast or french fried
All biscuits and cakes are denied
I can only dream
Of chocolate ice-cream
'Til my fat cells are de-toxified

INTERNET SHOPPING

I used to go out shopping
Now I never leave the house
I leave all the slogging
To my computer mouse

With designer shoes and holidays
And all things in between
Flashing there seductively
Upon my lap-top screen

Just tap in credit details
Send orders whizzing through the air
I've spent a bloody fortune
And I haven't left my chair

TWO POST-CODES

I'm flabby and fatter by loads
My bottom requires two post-codes
I'll not eat my dinner
I want to get thinner
Before my gut is bust and explodes

CLARA CORNFLAKE

Clara Cornflake had an ambition
She wanted to go on a deep-sea mission
She hired a boat and an acqua-lung
What a pity she forgot the bung

Clara waved 'Goodbye' and said 'So Long'
And started out with great aplomb
With nautical stance she set the sail
And with her bucket she started to bale

Quickly day turned into night
And Clara baled with all her might
But at the time she thought of quitting
She met an octopus doing his knitting

He knitted a rope so stout and strong
Just the job to tow Clara along
The water was up to Clara's knees
She abandoned the boat for water-skies

Clara dropped the rope but still kept going
And bumped into a jelly-fish doing his sewing
He threw her a line from a reel of cotton
But Clara missed and sank to the bottom

And there upon the ocean bed
She met her own true love, and wed
Kenneth Kipper, and they were able
To be together on the breakfast table

SAND OF SHAME

Why are they doing this to me?

My fear intensifies as I see the howling mob surrounding me
Their faces contorted into a grotesque mask
Absorbing a sensuous pleasure from my torture and humiliation
Empty-headed women in white stiletto sandals
Men, faces beaded with sweat, mouths gaping
Their eyes feed upon the violent acts of bestiality

In a profusion of pain I sink once more to my knees
The blood runs freely from my severed shoulder muscles
It congeals in the hot sand
I can no longer lift my head
My executioner stands before me

There is no escape from the bull-ring
And the ultimate obscenity

GIVE THANKS

I've a yearning to be a Size Ten
It's Ryvita and lettuce 'til then
I'll have such thin thighs
When I give up pork pies
I'll say "Thank You God" and "Amen"

THE 'PLEB' SEX

I've always found it useful
To have a man about the house
For dealing with the spiders
Or if the cat brings in a mouse

For sorting out the plumbing
Scraping gunge from all the drains
And cleaning out the gutters
When it rains, and rains, and rains

So please don't make us equal
I know I couldn't cope
For the mundane things of life you need
A plucky little bloke

SPENCER

There was an accountant called Spencer
Whose IQ was rated by Mensa
It came well below
The tea-lady called Flo
Now he's the refreshment dispenser

LOVE TALK

Each night he says "Hi, darling,
And how are you today?"
He says "You are my little love
Shall we go out to play?"

"Your eyes are brown and beautiful
You're a sweetie and so cute
And I don't mind your brown curls
All over my new suit!"

My eyes light up excitedly
And go misty – like a fog
But then my ego crumples
'Cos he's talking to the dog!

NOT HIS FAULT

It's the teachers' fault
They don't understand him
It's the other boys' fault
They lead him astray
It's the television's fault
Puts ideas into his head
It's the policeman's fault
Always picking on him
It's the old woman's fault
Dying when he hit her

Never his fault
Said his Mother

CHANGES

The new born Spring and balmy breeze
That supersedes the Winter's freeze
Warm Summer sun-shine on my face
The raindrops on a spider's lace

The sparkly frost on grass at night
In ghostly gleam of pale moon-light
Virgin white – untrodden snow
The silver lining grey clouds show

Autumn's drift of russet golds
The wonderment of earth unfolds
The red of sun-set's powerful glory
Seasonal changes – never-ending story

The peace of dawn, so still, so silent
The power of storms, contrary, violent
Then by dusk and star-light's grace
The world is calmed by night's embrace

THE INVIGILATOR

By the end of today my fate will be sealed
My palms itch with sweat and fear shakes me
I hold myself silent and look straight ahead
It's not yet revealed what awaits me

Gimlet eyed, po-faced, women survey me
They have soft soled, brogue shoes on their feet
They creep up and peer over my shoulder
Making sure there is no chance to cheat

For months I have anguished, prepared and revised
Studied hard with no time to revel
The Invigilator says "Now you may start"
I'm doing my Pure Maths 'A' level

DOG'S DINNER

I'm busy working in the kitchen
Grumpy-Guts comes home – he's late
He says "Wotcha, where's me dinner?"
He expects it waiting on a plate

You weren't here at the time you said
So don't start to smack your lips
I gave your rump-steak to the dog
And you've got egg and chips

KILLING TIME

It's cold and dark and rats abound
One o'clock – four hours to go
And I must write my letters now
In the shaded torch-light glow

Dearest Mother, in my mind I see
Your sweet face as clear as day
I long to rest upon your breast
Have you wipe my fears away

The time creeps by, it's two a.m.
Dear Friend, to you I write
Rest easy in your Blighty bed
Before you're re-called to fight

We've stood together side by side
Faced bayonet and shell
Like brothers lived these muddy months
Through unrelenting bloody hell

My watch shows now it's nearly three
To my love, my joy, my wife
I pen thoughts of bitter sadness
I'll not be there to share your life

My Darling, it's been bare a year
And so long we've been apart
So great the love I feel for you
That I write with breaking heart

Bestow a kiss on our beloved child
And, as always, now I pray
You'll be delivered safely
Of the babe that's on the way

Do not spend your life in grief
But remember me each day
And berate the inept generals
Who threw our lives away

At four – the final letter
To address humanity
When you view the grave-side crosses
See not just a name, see me

I do not give my life gladly
But in duty I am strong
With courage I face carnage
While the generals get it wrong

At five o'clock the whistle blows
And o're the top we run
To face machine gun bullets
That kill another mother's son

Upon me now death's cool embrace
Out here in no-man's land
A generation wasted
Like time and drifting sand

BOBBY BUNFACE

Bonny Bobby Bunface had chips for tea each day
Piled on top of burgers, made him too fat to play
But Bobby was a bright lad, he needed to get fitter
He wanted to know what to do and asked his friends on Twitter
They said "Stick to Healthy Eating and slimmer you will get
Chuck out all the junk food and eat the alphabet"

A for apricot and apple sweet
B for banana - unzip it and eat
C is for cauliflower or cabbage green
D is for damsons (delicious with cream)
E for the energy food gives to you
F for some figs and a trip to the loo
G is for grapefruit with cherry on top
H is for haricot beans eaten hot
I is for ice-cream (an occasional treat)
J for the junk food that's best not to eat
K is for kiwi with prickly skin
L is for lettuce (but slugs live within)
M is for melon and mango exotic
N for nuts, crack the shell and you've got it
O for orange, you just choose which type
P is for pears or for plums when they're ripe
Q is for quince which is quite hard to find
R is for rhubarb cooked soft with no rind
S is for swede which is good in a stew
T for tomato with lovely red hue

U for unfit – don't get flabby and fat
V for variety will save you from that
W for wisdom and words full of truth
X for the exercise to maintain your youth
Y for the YES you will shout with great zeal
Z for the zing in your life that you feel

So Bobby Bunface did his best, to pork pies he said "Goodbye"
He ate and ate the alphabet - now he's a super fit cool guy

NAOMI

Again I see those chocolate eyes
Shining, full of love and life
She's never known starvation
Faced death, destruction, strife

She gently takes my hand in hers
Says: Come on, Nana, come
We want you here beside us
Me, and Dad, and Mum

In her eyes my mind reflects the years
So long ago, but clear
To the time of my first meeting
With her Mum I hold so dear

To a war-zone called Rwanda
I'd travelled miles in dust and heat
I'd bribed and greased so many palms
To adopt the child I'd yet to meet

They took me to a dingy room
The paint-work peeled and bare
And on a grubby mattress
An abandoned child lay there

They said her name's Naomi
She two, or perhaps three
She doesn't come with paper-work
In this hostile territory

She's scarred and thin and very frail
Survivor of the genocide
She turned her head to face me
Dark eyes, fear-filled and wide

She stood within the cot rails
Her little body bare
She raised her arms towards me
And I loved her, then and there

I wrapped her in a blanket
But my heart filled with despair
I could take Naomi with me
But leave so many there

So with my adopted daughter
I fled the country with this waif
I vowed her my protection
And a home secure and safe

And now so many years have passed
She's a family of her own
And our love for each other
Never faltered, only grown

But I remember our first meeting
And those eyes of chocolate brown
When I grabbed Naomi in my arms
And we left that shanty-town

We still see war-zones on the telly
The hideous mass slaughter
But each day I thank the stars above
For Naomi – my daughter

SIMPLE RHYME

I don't write clever poetry
Rhyming drivel, yes, that's me
And when you've read the stuff I've writ
You can wrap your chips in it

Short Stories

THIRD CHOICE

He was still screaming but it didn't matter anymore. In her mind she had abdicated all responsibility for him. She had not bothered to pull back the curtains that morning and the darkness of the bedroom cocooned her. Now the decision had been made she was strangely calm.

She chewed another bitter tablet. Her thoughts wandering, sometimes with surprising clarity, sometimes confused. For so long she had struggled. Life before Michael belonged to another existence. Nobody understood what it was like; the constant tiredness, the relentless battle day in day out with a fractious child who screamed incessantly for hours on end.

She had no family nearby and Philip didn't care. "Pull yourself together," he'd said. "For God's sake, pull yourself together. Get the doctor to give you something." He didn't know what it was like. He left it all behind each day.

Only that morning Sandra had sat in the doctor's waiting-room. She liked Dr. Blackwood. He was older, he would understand what she was going through; didn't he have children of his own? She could talk to him.

Her eyes gazed at the dozens of notices on the waiting-room wall, but she didn't consciously see them, it was just somewhere to look. The buzzer sounded and she heard her name called. She remembered the shiny tiles on the floor which blurred now as once again the tears started, even before she knocked on the surgery door.

The doctor scrolled up her notes on the computer screen. "Ah, Mrs. Er Er Umm. Now, now, what's all this about?" The doctor thrust a tissue into her hand. "Buck up, buck up, that's the ticket." One avuncular hand patter her shoulder, the other tapping in the name of some mind-numbing drug on the keyboard in front of him. "Just a little something to settle you down, my dear," he said, his moon-shaped face beaming at her, his eyes not quite meeting hers. "Soon have you right. Quite normal, just a touch of post-natal depression, everyone gets it. Hormones you know. Nothing to worry about."

Sandra took the printed-out prescription and tried to speak. Dr. Blackwood's hand was already on the buzzer for the next patient. She turned and went out of the surgery. Closing the door quietly behind her, she leant back against it. She realised with incredulity that she had not spoken a single word throughout the whole consultation.

Sandra collected Michael, now sleeping soundly. She knew she shouldn't leave him outside; anybody could have walked off with him. Perhaps that was what she wanted – never to have to cope with him again. She grabbed the handles of the baby-buggy and, with shoulders slumped, walked towards the chemist. She kept her eyes down avoiding contact with anyone.

The assistant took the prescription. "You're exempt, aren't you?" she said briskly, eyeing the baby. "You must fill this in." Sandra ticked one of the boxes, signed her name and passed it back. "Five minutes," the assistant said. "It will be five minutes." Sandra looked at her blankly. "Haven't you got any shopping to do?"

Sandra sat down. She didn't know if she needed any shopping or not. Soap – yes, she needed soap. It was all there, bars of it, on the shelf in front of her. All different prices and brands. Sandra felt the familiar panic when faced with making a decision. The assistant called her and handed her a neat little bag containing the pills.

Sandra didn't remember walking home. She only remembered entering the kitchen and Michael starting to scream again. She knew she should change him and feed him, but she'd reached the end. She couldn't do it anymore. Slowly she dragged herself upstairs and, without undressing, got into bed.

The tablets were hard to take without water, but she couldn't face going back into the kitchen to get a glass. Was it the fourth or fifth she was chewing now? Bile rose in her throat. It wasn't as though she actually wanted to die, she just didn't want to live and there was no third choice.

Suddenly, a number she had seen in the surgery waiting-room just a short while ago leapt into her mind. A number that was easy to remember. Desperately her hand reached for the telephone by the bed and, with shaking fingers, she pressed each digit. She got through. The harsh sounds of her raucous sobs echoed loudly along the 'phone-line but it didn't matter. The person at the other end would wait for her. At last there would be someone to share her suffering, never condemning, never criticising. Just listening and understanding. They would come. They would take her and Michael in their arms and comfort them both.

She heard the life-saving words – "Samaritans here, can we help you?" There was a third choice. Sandra had found it.

TEUTONIC CHALLENGE

Frau Acht-Beinen was glad they'd decided to spend their holiday here in Germany. She'd seen pictures of the swimming pool and en-suite bathrooms in a travel magazine somebody had left laying around. It hadn't been an easy journey, quite some drain, but now they were settled in a nice undisturbed corner of the hotel it had all been worthwhile.

She lay quite still admiring the silky smoothness of her husband's sleek body before nudging him awake. "Fritz", she whispered "you'll have to be quick". "Use the towel. Reserve your spot".

Fritz stretched and rubbed the web of sleep from his eyes. Within second he had disentangled himself from her marital clasp, crept from the corner and headed for the towel carelessly left hanging down over the edge to dry from the night before. He clambered up to claim his spot and bask in the patch of sunlight on the tiled surround. Then, taking a deep breath, he slid into the ceramic depth. He had made it; he was first.

Nor far away Norman Greensleeves was also waking up; his half-raised lids revealing bloodshot eyes. He too fought the entanglement of sleep, albeit without much fervour and hampered by the eight pints of Pina Colada sloshing about dangerously within his ample paunch. After yesterday spent in the sun ogling nubile frauleins laying on towels around the pool, his body resembled a 'past its sell-by date' baked bean.

Norman lumbered from the bed and morosely rummaged for his towel. All he could think of was the luxury of submerging his burning body in cool water. Apart from a couple of burps and the odd obnoxious effluvium he was careful not to wake his wife – he didn't think his head could stand Hilda's invective just at the moment. He staggered through the door – this time, he thought, I'll be first.

"Hilda," he shrieked, "that bloody spider's in the bath again!"

Fritz gathered his eight legs together, clicked his heels and smartly goose-stepped towards the plug-hole!

HOT-LINE TO HEAVEN

Our Heavenly Father ever wise, with his grey beard and halo, played through his own pre-recorded message on the answer-phone. His voice was carefully disguised against the dismay he felt when dealing with his angel-staff and the earth-bound mortals he had created in his own image. People didn't like this new idea. For six days of the week they had a direct line to God; on the seventh they got his answer-phone. Even Heavenly Fathers need a day of rest. God reached for the aspirin, gave his harp a quick twang, and prepared to listen.

"Hello there, boss", the thick Irish brogue of Angel-006-and-Three-Quarters had God clutching the edge of his throne. Angel-006-and-Three-Quarters never quite got anything right. God gulped a couple of aspirin with a swig of holy water and held tight to his halo to prevent it slipping.

"It was like this, sir. You remember how I dented me wing falling off the scales during Holy Weight Watchers Week when I'd been on the Guinness; well, I was on me way to get it straightened out at the Wonky Wing Repair Parlour when I got caught up in this riot in the Bog End Road. There I was, wingless, up against this tattooed 'paddy' with a crew cut who was legless and chucking petrol bombs all over the place. Well now, thinking and ducking at the same time don't come easy, and the flaming glass splinters were creating havoc with the ruffle round me loin cloth, so I waved me wand and changed his bottles to plastic – I forgot plastic melts, begorrah! Sorry God, but he's on his way up!"

God paused the answer-phone, sent down a crack of thunder over Luton to relieve his tension, and reached for his pad of re-direction forms. 'Dear Red', he wrote. 'Am sending another one down. Don't bother to light the fire, he's bringing his own'. God's hand also hovered over the pile of secondment forms. Perhaps he could get Angel-006-and-Three-Quarters transferred to the opposition.

God, his composure restored to that befitting his position, switched the answer-phone back on, and then wished he hadn't. Immediately the disgruntled tones of his Secretary-Angel-63-42-63 assaulted his ears. God never wanted Angel-63-42-63 for his secretary. That was a big mistake made by his dyslexic Recruitment-Angel. God distinctly asked for Secretary-Angel-36-24-36. Look what had happened only last week when the heavenly choir was due to sing for the Home for Wayward Women of Wigan and the unicorns went on strike and wouldn't pull the chariots. (They wanted to change their horse blankets for Laura Ashley duvet covers). I'll call up a fleet of taxi drivers, she'd said. Only Secretary-Angel-63-42-63 could spell TAXIS as TAXES. The next thing God had was half the Inland Revenue throwing their bowler hats over the Pearly Gates and Saint Peter 'phoning for the Samaritans.

God pressed the fast forward button until he got to the next message. The booming tones of ex-Guards dyslexic Recruitment-Angel-1001 shook Cloud Nine on which God was sitting, sending a shower of hailstones, the size of golf-balls, scattering over Blimpton-on-Mud, causing havoc with the bells of the Morris dancers performing on the pier. "You remember you ordered a troupe of Lady-Cleaning-Angels with high morale to clean up after the Cherubs Boxing Night Binge. Well, I mixed up high and low, and Secretary-Angel-63-42-63 typed MORALS instead of MORALE". There was a pause – apprehension rose – "There's a group of ladies at the gate, all wearing red hats and no knickers."

God pressed the stop button and took another aspirin. With all these administrative problems the 'phone must seem permanently engaged to earth-bound mortals. There were still three more messages on the tape. What was the time? God looked at his sundial – he could never get the stupid thing to work in the dark, so he looked at his Rolex instead. Still another couple of hours before he was live on-air again.

He re-started the answer-phone and groaned. Oh no! Not Matron-Angel-9999. What had the cherubs been up to now! God couldn't believe his ears. Cherubs were definitely not what they used to be. He could remember them in years gone by, their plump little pink unisex bodies playing hide and seek with the puffy white clouds. And now what was Matron saying? They'd traded in their flutes for a set of drums and a base guitar, and Leader-Teenage-Cherub has had his ears pierced! Matron went on, somewhat hysterically. "That's not all. They've painted their wings in psychedelic purple and are holding an Acid Heaven Party."

God was beginning to wish he'd never had this answer-phone installed. It was certainly the daftest invention he'd ever allowed to happen. He heard about computer viruses; the next invention must be an answer-phone virus that could travel down all the 'phone lines simultaneously; that would keep the earth-bound wiz-kids occupied for a while!

God listened once again as the strangled tones of an earthling in high dudgeon came on the line. "Mick here." 'Oh God', thought God: 'It's spotted Mick, the mugger from Tooting!' (When he had learnt the error of his ways God would do something about his acne). He listened attentively to his earth-bound caller.

"Look 'ere, God. Just leave it out, will ya? All we do is a bit of shove and push, some smash and grab on the side. Now there's not much evil intent in that, is there? So what's happening to us. Just look at Stanley. Went to mug this nice little old lady, when she ups and clobbers him round the ear 'ole with a bottle of Syrup of Figs. I ask ya! If Stanley had a brain it could have been damaged."

God listened patiently while Mick went on. "And as for Norman! Well, you didn't have to set him up like that on his first mugging, did ya? Got a victim well staked out in the lift of Ombingo House – you know the one – high-rise in Clapham – yeah, well, what happens? Lift got jammed and Norman spent three days banged up with a Sumo Wrestler practicing macramé with his legs. The 'orspital is still trying to untangle him." God grinned. Holy Anti-Mugging Week was certainly taking effect.

"And look what you did to our Elvin," Mick continued. "There was this girl with a pushchair – easy target see – so Elvin says 'Give us yer purse, darlin', or I'll take the kid', and next thing, there's Elvin standing in the middle of the road, covered in prune puree, holding a screaming baby. Young mother? – oh yeah – she legged it and was last seen on a Number Eleven bus heading for Shepherds Bush. No sense of responsibility, young mothers, nowadays. Wot's worse, Elvin's had to spend all last week's mugging money on Paddi-Pants and dried milk powder!"

God doubled up with glee – caught his halo with his foot as it slipped off and flipped it back into place. (I mean, well, you've got to have a bit of decorum when you're in that position, haven't you? What if the cherubs saw him throwing his halo in the air and dancing round the answer-phone). God considered carefully – what could he do next week when Holy Anti-Mugging Week was over? Thoughts about a come-uppance for litter-louts and boy-racers flashed through his mind.

The answer-phone clicked with its final message. "Wonky Wing Repair Parlour here, Guv. Could you tell Angel-006-and-Three-Quarters that his wings are ready." God switched off the answer-phone – it had done a good day's work. There was one thing for sure though, his flock certainly still needed him. God threw the odd beam of sunshine in the direction of Blackpool, and prepared to go live again.

FLORRIE

She watched as another fly stuck to the length of sticky paper hanging from the ceiling. A draught from a window made the bakelite shade of the single bulb move slightly. All around the walls the rim of shadow tilted. Slowly, with one finger, she traced the outline of a flower on her wrap-around apron. The print had faded over the years and the garment had assumed an all over greyish colour. Her hands were bent, the knuckles knobbly with arthritis. She surveyed them mournfully and ran one grimy finger-nail under another in a perfunctory cleaning motion.

"Bugger Hitler," she swore under her breath. If it wasn't for that devil bombing the gas main in East Street she could at least have made a cup of tea.

With much effort she levered herself out of the chair and lumbered across to the table. On the centre of the table was a loaf from which Florrie cut herself a chunk. She stabbed the slice viciously with a long-handled metal toasting fork and held it to the blaze. The smell of toasting bread filled the room. Florrie took the earthenware pot of pork dripping from the stone ledge in the larder and spread it generously on the hot toast.

"Oh Yes, Mr. Hitler, you and your army couldn't stop me getting those pork knuckles," she muttered with grim satisfaction. Over an hour she had queued for them, but it had been worth it. The grease ran down the deep lines from the corner of her mouth. Florrie closed her eyes, patted her ample stomach and belched contentedly.

THE FINAL ACT

My fellow travelling companion lies desolate in the corner. The straw tucked round her is fetid: urine soaked, wet and dried again and again. Our journey is interminable as we are jostled and jolted in the semi-darkness of our cage. But tonight is mine. Tonight will culminate in the purpose of my tortured existence.

My eyes water in the blazing light but I don't need sight. Feeling is all I need. Hate seethes within me. The sequined coat of the ring-master shoots slivers of pain inside my head. This time I will cower, but not in fear. No more will the King of the Beasts submit to the exploitation of man.

I know the beat of the music and I turn and balance on my stool; my mate anticipating my movements. The whip is raised and I am ready. The music crescendos as I spring. At last my tormentor becomes the tormented.

YELLOW STREAK

Fear is a funny thing. Funny peculiar that is. Well, I mean, you expect people to get a bit worried about some things – Income Tax or getting the 'flu, for example; and fear might cause the odd tremor of an earring on an Arsenal supporter at an away game with Sheffield Wednesday; but you don't expect gas men to be reduced to quivering wrecks at the drop of a hat, do you?

Just picture the old fashioned image of your average gas man. The species only came in two varieties anyway. There was the type with long fingers, peaked cap and short pencil, who wore the hand-me-down uniform of a seven-foot giant on his four-foot frame. And then there's the other sort: six feet wide, with buttons straining over the reservoir commonly known as a 'beer-belly'. The abject terror instilled in this second variety was all the fault of our ginger cat, aptly named Tom.

Being a sporty sort of cat he liked to do the odd spot of big-game hunting en route from his fishing trips in next door's pond and sometimes, after being out on the tiles all night, he brought me home a little present. At bit like my other half in that respect! Anyway, gift of the day was a mouse which was deposited just of centre on the kitchen floor. Discovering it still had all its legs, 'Mouse' used them to great advantage, dived under the cupboard door and ended up sitting at the back of the central heating boiler on top of the gas jets which were likely to come on at any moment!

Well, being a humane sort of person and not relishing the thought of roast mouse wafting through the warm air central heating system for ever more, I made a bee-line for the thermostat and switched it off.

With galloping hypothermia, not to mention frozen extremities, Tom and I lay on our stomachs and watched 'Mouse' basking in the warmth of the pilot light. Never one for spectator sports, Tom soon got fed-up and took himself off to sleep in the airing cupboard. With chattering teeth and hot-water-bottle, I called the gas man!

He arrived, complete with sausage fingers, clutching a metal tool box and deposited half a ton of mud on the hall carpet. Desmond – that's what he said his name was – lay down on the floor and peered into the depth of the gas boiler. Well, I say 'lay', actually he sort of rocked on the 'reservoir' previously mentioned.

"What have you got stuck in there?" "It's a mou….." I didn't get any further. If sheer terror can move mountains it certainly moved Desmond with an alacrity I would not have thought possible for a man of his shape. He backed towards the kitchen door, his face ashen and beaded with sweat. He struggled to speak. "Nnnnno, No," he stuttered. "Nnnnn … not on your nelly, darlin'. I'm not going near there." "It's only a little mouse," I ventured.

Desmond clutched his head, pleaded instant migraine and sat down heavily on the nearest kitchen chair. "Look," I reasoned, handing him a cup of hot, sweet tea, "it's hardly likely to go for your throat with fangs bared, now is it?"

"You look 'ere, missus," (I'd stopped being darlin'), "I'm a fitter, not a rodent catcher. It's not my job to catch mice."

"If you don't get it out, I'll report you to the Gas-Board, the RSPCA and Cowards Anonymous!" That stopped him in his tracks. He peered again into the boiler. "Look," I smiled ingratiatingly at him, "just undo a few screws and things and I'll get the mouse out." A brainwave hit me. "I know, you can wear my Marigold gloves!"

I passed him the yellow rubber gloves and he squeezed his podgy fingers into them. Sweating profusely, eyes wide with fear, and breathing rapidly, he advanced with his screw-driver at the ready. He undid the front panel, then retreated to the far corner of the kitchen, leaving me to scoop out a rather warm and bemused little mouse. "Don't let it near me," he gibbered, cowering behind the broom cupboard door. Carefully I carried the mouse to the bottom of the garden and dropped it over next door's fence. Desmond gathered his tools and headed towards the back door as fast as his fat little legs would carry him.

I turned up the thermostat and sat down to thaw out with a steaming cup of tea. Now it was my turn to be frightened. Just how much would the Gas-Board charge for the removal of a mouse from the central heating boiler? I wondered if they would allow me a discount to replace the bright yellow rubber gloves that even now were fearfully clutching the steering wheel as Desmond drove away.

True Story
Only the names have been changed to protect the innocent
Today's Gas-Men are much more up-market!

GHOST FOX

I'm not exactly looking forward to dying; I know it will be savage and brutal. It wouldn't be so bad if I could depart this life peacefully in my den with my cubs growing up around me in the safety of nature's embrace. No, my end will be barbaric and violent, in a frenzy of blood-lust. But ... I could just about cope with the thought of dying if it were possible to come back to this sad earth as a ghost in human form.

My mind does backward somersaults with glee as I perceive the mischief I could produce by joining a gathering of 'the unspeakable in pursuit of the uneatable'. The power to diminish their pomposity and arrogance would be within my grasp. All my fox-friends around the country would find extracts from the following live radio commentary on the local hunt amusing – with a little ghostly help from me!

"..... And here comes Lady Amelia Ploddington-Wallop. She's racing her mount towards Hawthorn Hedge in close pursuit ..... Oops ..... Oh dear! The horse stopped so suddenly you'd have thought it had seen a ghost. Pity Lady Amelia didn't. Game girl; she gallantly took the jump head first. Her ample proportions are now firmly wedged in the boggy patch. I can see an ambulance, closely followed by a mobile crane, arriving on the scene.

.....There seems to be some sort of problem at the far end of the field. Colonel Whatnot-Blimp, still firmly seated, is minus his horse. Seems that some unseen hand has spread super-glue liberally on his saddle. If something isn't done quickly a walk like that could become a permanent affliction. I can see a first-aider rushing towards him.

..... In the distance is Dame Daphne Chatterley-Flogit, named side-saddle rider of the year in the publication 'Mount and Whippet', thundering across the buttercup meadow. She has declined to be

interviewed about rumours regarding her recent activities involving her game-keeper and a riding-crop.

..... Aah, now there's a flurry of activity behind the privet hedge. Is it the fox? No ... No ... It's Mrs Peacock-Gripe. I'm informed by a reliable source that she's been stuck in her outsize jodhpurs for the last six hours with a zip that mysteriously refuses to budge. Is that why she's standing crossed-legged? At this very moment she's frantically running the blade of a Stanley Knife up the straining seams ..... Ooh dear me! What a nasty accident. I can see the vicar's wife running over to her with a blanket.

..... Events here are going from bad to worse. Somehow a handful of 'doggy-chocs' has found its way into Squire Littlejohn-Pugh's trouser pocket. The hounds are going mad. It's not being helped by two rottweilers and a ferret joining in the fracas. Oh dear, Oh dear ..... What a very messy scene. That will certainly curb his blood-lust, and any other type of lust, for a while! A squad car from the local constabulary is racing across the field.

..... Let's join the hunt further on. Ah, now we see Wayne Bloggs, lottery winner and member of the 'nouveau riche', leading the field. I've never seen anything like it! Wayne has over-taken the fox and is still racing on. It's as if an unseen force is pursuing the horse – they're heading for the river ..... Oh dear, Oh dear. What a good job horses can swim. Pity about Wayne – he only came along to ingratiate himself with the Ploddington-Wallops.

..... What a day, what a day! The chase has finally been abandoned with most of the hunters being transported to the local hospital. It's alleged that laxatives and sleeping pills were added to the Stirrup Cup. The police have so far failed to apprehend the perpetrators of this heinous deed.

..... *Major Aubrey Bogit-Pong has been incarcerated in a mobile field port-a-loo for several hours now. A late news flash from our reporter at the scene has revealed that the Red Cross has arranged a parachute drop of emergency rations.*

..... *What a truly sporting occasion this has been .....* "

Yes, being a ghost could bring justice, not to mention 'come-uppance', to supporters of this orgy of cruelty. If it were thugs disembowelling a domestic cat belonging to the pensioner next door on a council estate they would be branded for what they really are. If it's the 'well-healed' hypocrites of our society doing the same thing it's called 'Sport'.

Until my turn comes, I must continue to live by outwitting them!

TILTING THE BALANCE

Henry was 'clock-watching'. In just under an hour he would be off for the weekend. In just under a week, he would be 'off' for the rest of his life. Henry had worked for the Pensions' Office for forty-one years and, although he and Amy had never exactly enjoyed riotous living, it had provided them with a steady income. Oh yes, very steady. Now it would provide them with a steady pension. Henry had been careful with his money over the years. He had also invested in a lump-sum endowment which was due to mature at the time of his retirement.

It was a quarter to five. In fifteen minutes he could leave his brown and cream painted office. He and Amy planned to spend one last weekend in their little green coloured caravan which, for the past thirty-four years, had stood in a field overlooked by the Surrey downs. He'd be sorry to give up the old 'van, but he knew Amy hankered after a newer model. She'd talked endlessly about electrical hook-ups, luxury shower fittings and modern 'cassette' toilets ever since they'd walked around their local showrooms. Henry had done some careful calculations. Yes, the endowment would provide just enough money to buy a new caravan outright.

Amy was also 'clock-watching'. It was five o'clock. In precisely twenty minutes Henry would be home. She sat down and mentally ticked off all the items she needed for their weekend. She too would be sorry to see the old 'van go, they had spent so many carefree days in it. They loved the countryside, seeing the seasons change from dewy Spring to golden Autumn. How often she'd watched rabbits playing in the dawn light and marvelled at the sun setting in a blaze of red glory over the Surrey hills. Oh yes, it had provided some happy times. Amy picked up her knitting and packed it in the big canvas hold-all just as Henry turned into the drive.

At six-fifteen Amy and Henry climbed into their ageing, well cared for, Ford and set off into the evening sunshine. "Last time, Old Girl," said Henry affectionately. Amy didn't answer. 'Old Girl' rankled a bit. She surveyed her grey hair in the mirror on the sun visor and patted a tightly permed curl into place. Amy was sixty-three to Henry's sixty-five. 'Oh well' she thought, 'perhaps he's right.' She smiled back at him. "Yes, but it'll be nice to have a new 'van after all this time."

They'd talked quite a lot about the new caravan. Of course, having electricity would mean they could park it on a modern site with electrical hook-ups. "Perhaps nearer the coast," said Henry. "Eastbourne would be nice. Yes, Eastbourne." They had always liked Sussex and now they were free they could travel just that little bit further afield. Henry glanced at his watch. "Six thirty-five", he said. "If there's not too much traffic on the M25 we could be there by eight o'clock." Amy settled back in her seat anticipating a glass of sherry in the late evening sunlight.

At five to eight Henry, manoeuvring the car through the gates of the field, came to an abrupt halt. He and Amy stared in horror at the litter-strewn scene before them. Between a battered car and a heap of rotting rubbish stood their little green painted caravan, its usual neatly curtained windows stripped bare. It was a while before either Henry or Amy spoke. Then ... "Squatters," exclaimed Henry indignantly. "We've got squatters."

They got out of the car and cautiously approaching the open door, were stopped in their tracks by the bizarre sight of a skinny youth sitting on the step. His head was shaved except for a red Mohican style cock's comb running from front to back. He stared indolently at them. Almost immediately he was joined by three others. Another man of huge proportions and two young women. The second man had shaved his head on one side only and on this was the tattoo of a purple dragon. His stomach bulged grotesquely over the studded belt of his leather trousers. The two women were dressed in black. One was blonde with roots matching her dress; the other had jet black, spiky hair and blue painted lips giving her pale face a sinister appearance. Henry motioned to Amy to stand behind him.

"What d'yer want?" snarled Red Mohican. Henry tried to face him bravely. "What do you think you're doing?" his voice squeaked. "This is my caravan. What are you all doing here?"

Purple Dragon stepped over his squatting companion. "F... off," he said, his tone menacing. Henry took a step backwards. "Now you look here. You get out of my 'van'". He tried to sound authoritative. Amy, her eyes peeping from behind Henry's shoulder, braced herself to face the two men. "We'll call the police, that's what we'll do. They'll come and get you out of our 'van." Followed by Black Roots, Blue Lips stepped out of the caravan. "Push off, you silly old cow!" she said, pointing at Amy.

Henry and Amy retreated to the safety of their car and quickly locked the doors. Henry drove out of the gate and, turning the car swiftly, he parked it in the shadow of some trees only a few yards along the lane. There he and Amy sat in shocked silence for some time before a rare feeling of anger slowly surfaced within them. They could call the police, but didn't squatters have 'rights'? Sometimes the balance of the law seemed to tilt in the favour of the offender.

Shortly after nine o'clock Red Mohican and Purple Dragon drove out in their battered car. Henry and Amy edged forward under the cover of the trees until they had a clear view of the field. Within an hour the two men returned and unloaded a crate of beer and, from what Amy and Henry could see from the light of the caravan, a couple of bottles of spirits. Henry looked at his watch. It was now gone ten o'clock and quite dark. He and Amy sat back in their car seats and began to make plans ......

In the half-light of dawn Henry and Amy crept into the field and peered through the windows into the dim interior of the caravan. Empty bottles and half eaten food littered the table. Discarded clothing was jumbled all over the floor. Having drunk themselves into a stupor, the inhabitants sprawled in their various stages of undress across the caravan. Henry quietly opened the door of the 'van. He raised his eyebrows and averted his eyes from the bare tattooed bosom of Blue Lips. 'No need to expose Amy to that short of thing,' he thought. "You stand in the doorway, my dear, and hold the bag open," he instructed her. Silently he gathered up all their clothing and pushed it into the black plastic sacks Amy held open. The quartet still slept soundly. Taking a final look around the devastated 'van, his eyes alighted on what appeared to be a brand new portable colour television set. He allowed himself a wry smile as he picked it up. Between them they dragged the sacks of clothing to join the pile of rotting rubbish, and Henry carried the television carefully back to their car.

Fearfully now, as it was getting lighter, Henry made a second journey into the field. This time, sweating profusely, he removed the number plate and slowly wound up the legs of the caravan. The squatters still slept on. Once again he returned to the car. Now came the time when he would have to act with cool precision or all their plans would fail. Keeping the engine revs low he backed the car up to the caravan. With expertise gained through years of practice Henry coupled the 'van to the car. Amy, with equal speed, locked the 'van door and jammed one of her steel knitting needles into the ancient mechanism. With an alacrity which belied their years, Amy and Henry leapt into their car and, at breakneck speed, started off towards the field exit with the caravan bumping along behind them.

The inert bodies of the four inside hit the sides of the 'van with varying degrees of velocity. The initial impact of Black Roots landing squarely on the ample proportions of Purple Dragon brought forth the first reverberating explosion of expletives. The side of the caravan hitting the gate post as it swerved through caused a cascade of empty beer bottles to fall with spectacular accuracy on to Red Mohican, while the blue fluid from the chemical toilet oozed seductively around the bare extremities of Blue Lips.

"What the hell's happening," squawked Purple Dragon. "It's the old geezer, he's hitched us up," squealed Red Mohican, tugging in vain at the door handle. The caravan swerved violently, lurching from one side of the road to the other, as Henry swung recklessly along the narrow deserted country lanes. A bottle of brown sauce, followed closely by an open packet of sugar, three eggs and a pint of milk, flew through the air spraying its contents indiscriminately over the four reeling inhabitants. Crockery from every cupboard hurtled around making painful contact when they failed to duck.

Henry braked hard at the junction of the lane. The table collapsed on top of Purple Dragon and Black Roots collapsed on top of the table. Blue Lips, now with her matching blue extremities, still bravely clung to the edge of the toilet door. The toilet, however, probably not being quite so brave, made an unscheduled stop when it hit the back of Red Mohican's knees and carried him the length of the caravan to join Purple Dragon and Black Roots. Henry accelerated away from the junction and the whole sorry tangle of contents and bodies catapulted to the other end of the 'van.

Purple Dragon was the first to crawl to the front window of the caravan, lever open the broken catch at one end and push his tattooed fingers through to grip the lower edge of the sill, his mouth opening and shutting incoherently. Amy turned in her seat to watch his contorted face at the window. "What shall we do, Henry?" she gasped. Henry's answer was to brake hard. As Purple Dragon's nose hit the window pane, Henry accelerated again, causing the window to jam shut on the podgy fingers, permanently underlining the letters spelling 'LOVE' on them. Amy heard the anguished yell over and above the chaos within the 'van. Red Mohican only once regained his feet appearing at the window, his face resembling a squashed tomato and his cock's comb flattened.

At six in the morning, Henry turned on to the M25 and shuddered to a halt on the hard shoulder. Before any of the woebegone four could find their feet, Henry had unhitched the 'van. Even working quickly Henry could see Purple Dragon lumbering to his feet and advancing, with a murderous gleam in his eye, through a pile of dented saucepans and broken china. Without stands the caravan wobbled precariously and, with the combined weight of Blue Lips, Black Roots and Red Mohican, just a touch from Henry tilted the balance and the 'van finally came to rest with its rear end on the concrete of the hard shoulder of the M25. For a final time, Purple Dragon slid to the far end, landing firmly on top of the other three.

Henry jumped back into the car and he and Amy drove off the motorway at the junction just under a mile away, across the intersection, and back down the other side to re-join the M25 in the other direction. They arrived back at the spot opposite the doomed caravan at exactly the same time as the police car pulled up. Amy wound down her window to get a clearer view. Henry got out of the car, opened the bonnet and leaned against it. "Overheating, I think," he winked at Amy. "Just have to stop for a minute to cool down. That's the trouble with old cars."

On the other side of the motor-way the bare hairy leg of Purple Dragon, followed by his corpulent body, ably assisted by a policeman, was being levered through the distorted window. Blue Lips and Black Roots followed through the same gap, each scantily clad in a selection of Amy tea-towels and dusters. Finally the second policeman levered open the caravan door. Red Mohican fell out on to the hard shoulder and, clutching the tattered remnants of his Union Jack boxer shorts, was hauled to his feet. Black Roots was jabbering at the policemen and gesticulating wildly at Henry and Amy parked opposite. As Blue Lips and Purple Dragon started to join in, Amy had the final satisfaction of seeing the handcuffs slapped on all four of them.

"Time to go, dear," Amy said gently to Henry. He looked at his watch. It was six thirty-five again! Henry, his stance erect, nonchalantly got back into the car. Amy gazed at him in unbounding admiration of his fearlessness. Ever cautious, he edged the car into the slow lane of the M25. "You know, my dear," he said to Amy, "maybe with the new caravan we could be a little more adventurous. Perhaps go to Spain even." Amy clapped her hands delightedly. "Do you think," she asked, glancing at their new acquisition on the back seat, "that the television will work in Benidorm?" Laughing fit to burst, Henry and Amy joined the fast lane of their retirement.

THE CARELESS MATCH

In a terrifying way it is beautiful. The sky reflecting the flames is blood red. But let the wind blow away from me because the pall of smoke emanating from the heart of the blaze is dense and choking, darkening the evening air with falling ash and fumes. The burnt out undergrowth crunches under foot. Just a few metres away the dry grass crackles and sparks and the damp moss sizzles as it emits its black, billowing cloud.

All around the rustling sound of terrified creatures as they turn, and turn again, in their panic to escape. Birds scream hysterically as they fight against the conflicting instincts of abandoning their young and their quest to escape.

The rabbit and hare dash hither and thither; unable to decide between entombment and flight. The larger animals crash through bushes and thickets to emerge in greater danger than before. Grass snakes squirm on the hot ground.

All around the forest blazes. The wind makes swirls of flame as it licks and teases the trees into submission. The flowers curl and die. With plops and splashes, branches fall and hiss in the stream, shattering its surface with ripples reflecting the flames.

I dive into my silent world beneath the water to safety. I am a beaver and can escape the nightmare.